PENDLE WI

GERALDINE MONK

KFS

NEWTON-LE-WILLOWS

Published in the United Kingdom in 2012
by The Knives Forks And Spoons Press,
122 Birley Street
Newton-le-Willows,
Merseyside,
WA12 9UN.

ISBN 978-1-907812-96-5

Acknowledgements:

Versions of these poems first appeared in *Interregnum*, Creation Books, 1994 and *Selected Poems*, Salt Publishing, 2003.

The cover features a sculpture entitled *Deer Ribs, Willow, Twine and Fishing Line*, which was created from found objects by the artist Ruth Carpenter. Her work can be seen exhibited in and around the Highwood Camping site:

www.highwoodcamping.co.uk.

CONTENTS

PREFACE

When I first began my research into the Pendle witches in 1984 it proved exceedingly difficult to unearth any serious literature on the subject. Like many Lancastrians I first heard of the witches through the oral tradition of local myths and legends which had been passed down through the centuries but trying to discover the reality behind the folklore was, at the time, a struggle. The handful of local guide books available tended to cloak uncomfortable reality with cartoon images of haggish women with pointy hats, pointy noses and broomsticks; the template witch so beloved by children. Harsh facts were tagged on or sketchily embedded in the jokey safety of harum-scarum fantasy and consumer-friendly witchery.

The complex reality of these unlucky hill people caught up in their time, belief systems, religious persecution and the ambitions of petty officials is infinitely more disturbing and compelling than the clichéd merchandise of the Halloween circus served up by today's supermarkets or the trite albeit entertaining motifs of Hammer Horror films. It became increasingly obvious that the truth behind this sad and messy episode from our past was an inconvenience few wanted to deal with.

Collusion and reinforcement of the oblique misogyny and class snobbery that ran through many of these narratives suggested that the octogenarian matriarchs Anne Whittle (Chattox) and Elizabeth Southern (Demdike) were indisputably witches because they were elderly peasant women whereas the gentlewoman Alice Nutter was almost always excused and explained away as being a Roman Catholic. This type of ill-considered value judgment was meted out and made more depressing by an unquestioning reiteration of such notions.

When I finally tracked down a dog-eared transcript of Thomas Potts' account of the witch trials in my local reference library (so rare at the time I was not allowed to borrow it) it was a revelation to read an eyewitness account. A real version of reality rather than a version of fantasy. So piece by piece, year by year I gathered as much information as I could for my series of poems on the Pendle witches and in 1994 it was published by Creation Books under the title *Interregnum*.

The original version of *Interregnum* contained one section based on autobiographical material and one concerned with people who had special connections to Pendle such as the founder of the Quaker movement George Fox, who had his vision on Pendle Hill and was also incarcerated in Lancaster Castle, and the poet Gerard Manley Hopkins who taught at Stonyhurst college in the shadow of Pendle. There was also a scattering of contemporary references and quotes from, for example, the Birmingham Six (tried at Lancaster Castle) and the wrongfully imprisoned Stefan Kiszko.

For this 400th commemorative edition I am reproducing the two sets of monologues, retaining the original idea of having one monologue under the popular folklore name, e.g. Squintin Lizzie, and the second under the birth name, e.g. Elizabeth Device. I have however altered the presentation so that the monologues are in pairs rather than in two different sections as in the original. I have also included three additional 'Chantcasters' monologues. It is worth noting that all the words in these three poems, bar three lines, are reworkings of poems which Gerard Manley Hopkins wrote whilst he was in residence at Stonyhurst College. I was spurred on to do this reworking by one of the guide book authors who had reproduced the rather fine three lined 'witches spell' and dismissed it as 'gobbledegook'. There was no recognition that the caprice of circumstance which can make the difference between being condemned to die as a witch or being celebrated as Jesuit poet-priest could be one of time, gender and class.

❁

Since I wrote *Interregnum* the study of the Pendle witches has changed beyond recognition, propelled by more serious research and by the advent of women's studies, with its revisionism of women's history. This is however counterbalanced, perhaps even more strongly than ever before, by the caricature witches now promoted by the tourist industry. The flesh and blood reality of the Pendle witches will always be mired in myth and legend but essentially they were ordinary people caught up in extraordinary circumstance from which there was no escape.

Geraldine Monk 2012

CHANTCASTERS

DEMDIKE SINGS

Wild air,
world-mothering air,
nestling me everywhere,
that's fairly mixed
with riddles
and is rife
in every least things life
and nursing element.

(Welcome in womb and breast
birth-milk draw like breath)

Do but stand
where you can lift your hand
skywards;
round four fingergaps
it laps
such sapphire-shot
charged, steeped sky will not
stain light.
Mark you this:
It does not prejudice
the glass-blue days
when every colour glows.

Each shape and shadow shows.

The seven or seven times seven
hued sunbeam will transmit.

Perfect.

Not alter it.

Chattox Sings

What we have lighthanded left
will have waked
and have waxed
and have walked
with the wind.

This side
that side hurling
while we slumbered.
Oh then
weary then why should we tread?
O why
are we so haggard at the heart
so care-coiled
care-killed
is there no frowning of these wrinkles
ranked wrinkles deep.

Down?

No waving off these most
mournful messengers
still messengers
sad and stealing.

(Hush there – only
not within seeing of the sun)

Resign them
sign them
seal them
send them
motion them with breath.

Whatever's prized and passes of us
everything that's fresh and
fast flying of us
seems to us sweet of us
and swiftly away with
done away with
undone.

So beginning
be beginning to despair.

O there's none, no no there's none:
with sighs soaring
soaring sighs deliver.
Them:
        Beauty-in-the-ghost.

All Sing

Three biters bitten:
Earth's eye.   Earth's tongue.   Earth's heart.
Our counterparts cleaved.   Wreathed.   Cloven.

This age and era's evil ills
dearly and dangerously sweet
delights buried deep.

Tell us where?
A wild web.
A wondrous robe.

Tell us where?
Our lungs must draw and draw
a hair
an eyelash
a care kept.

Where kept?
Where?
Tell us where?

Around the beating heart.

b-boom b-boom b-boom

In the fine flood.
In the deathdance in the blood.

OUT-THOUGHTS & REPLIES

...of CHATTOX...

As the hill imperceptibly steepened
and dimmed
the invisible squadrons
multiplied to
fever
pitch beating
deep and
crammed
against themselves and each
pitched
at the plagued
inner roof of my skull
browning
bruised with the spray
of ceaseless distress
trying to
out
to be aired and wing-ing.

It is the way of words –
to leave yet
to remain:
to breed in
absence:
in the immaculate
space of decay.

So my name
became
my curse (or vice versa
it doesn't really matter:
egg-chicken-chicken-egg-chickadee-
chickabiddy-biddychatter-chatterbox-
Chattox-

Chatter shivered
from my toothless mouth
and thin
senior citizen lips –
each word
(as is their way)
elbowing its turn
to shine and
astonish.

But only I was amazed
by my outbreaks of
quirky
metaphors and
unchallengeable leaps to
lucidity
at invention that beggared
hypocrisy
and most of all
at how my mind
could fold in on a

pure
unstressed monotone of
silence
when all around me
raged.

AKA ANNE WHITTLE

a deal more
crafty than
uz
they knew
things never
uttered
in words
arms length and
longer than a
think
thi med id up
with things never
born
till pushed and named
from their gobs
lying
withershins
they knotted uz proper
in tittle-tattle
&
chains
*
straight up they
crawled
between our brain-curls
and

pin-winkled out
ower
tight black slugs of
monosyllables

...of DEMDIKE...

My pictures of clay:
They were my art.
Not the pitch and toss of play or
Sunday pleasure painting
but the teasing of spirit into the
dumb foxed earth.

It was the best and finest art
(a speedy way to make or take a life)
I spiked it with droplets of wonder
to be drunk unwittingly by children
and bring small animals to rest...

...the crest of my days...my life...
solitary moments...by the banks of the
Ribble and Calder I sat me down and chuckled
and sometimes wept...but mostly screwed up
my face into balls of exquisite contentment.

Oh certainly the images cried.
It is the way of clay.
Wetness...oozing through fingers...
make-believe eyes running...
to the far-off alarm call of birds.

I dried them. Fixed them. Thornpricked them.
Then sat well back and waited for the
diabolical climate to heighten.
Obliterate.

AKA ELIZABETH SOUTHERN

Unification creates power. Creates remains.
Unification creates exclusion. Persecution.
Random cells need violence
to club and hang together –
          hang together! Ha!
Bloody comics in
great bonds of fear –
hate-baiting coagulated fear.

Their movement formed
our position.
We slid to the edge
without heaving
or flutter. Without motion or commotion.
We hadn't the learning
to read us right.

We hadn't the food
for big-boned words to
kick mule-like
the wisest fool.

The switch was on.
Our world span:
The centrifuge of
virulent plasma clotted

huddled.   detached.
and made us
thin pale
      we
running down our
sparrow-boned
      legs.

...of ALICE...

Flapping wildly in
cloud broods
move and roost of hill rain
I never tired of.

Getting high caught
in mist-loops
steering my determined straight on
into unchoreographed circles
and the confused same spot.

White.   Sightless.   Bafflement.
Thickening animal throats
mutating child   man   woman
and the half-faced apparitions
stained sliver of eye
meeting sliver of I in
the glare of mutual suddenness.

And when it lifted?
It gathered excuse and
withdrew my license for the
welling-up of unspeakable wow!
Consorting with elements:
fractious, undesirable,
contra, alive. The pit

against pit of rootless
ease. The feed for my ungovernable
core to help me fight the regime of
mealtimes and the stifling niceties
inbetween
called 'life'.

AKA ALICE NUTTER

Alice through the centuries
of unrecorded silence.
That is my story:

Your bedtime night-night
fairy tales fill
cells
with injury
hurt the heart and
bleed the kick from
words
hanging limp from my
lips
those perfectly wrought
curlicues of sentences
dripped to my feet.

Sound spirited away.   Unwrit
forever
my inconvenient reasoning
my one stab at life
cut....

…of 'Mouldheels'…

I swear
folk dropped dead either side
of curse – they have a tendency to –
we didn't invent mortality
death came regardless
but the mind slavers – turns cannibal –
chance is connected – devoured
throats hurt – constrict
the inflamed lump of raw foresight –
swallow and keck
swallow and keck
keck.

Unfussed as always the
dead bled fresh blood –
I swear
they needed no encouragement from us –
willingly – with gasp
the shrieking and the
foul yelling
sucked out
long
at last.

AKA KATHERINE HEWIT

It hurt.   Being
felled by a blunt brain.
A nincompoop
pokin iz nosey
wi manicure nails
tapered to cynical infinity:
Pin pointy dead onz.
Ten witherin sticks to taunt.

E was nowt budda Jimmy-bum-licker.
E lived down't lane in a big owse
wi iz porky fatted fingers drippin
rings and blottin copy
after nervous copy – and for what?
A right royal smile?
The patronising smirk of
ultimate noble birth to charm iz drab
and impotent circle.

A could ave pushed iz super up
for't grief and sufferin e set in motion
and time trapped eternity.
A could ave done a lot o things – hypothetically –
with water mirrors and half moons A could ave
gagged the snotty little bugger
talkin down iz nose
talkin do-dah-lah-di like
talking do-dah-lah-di.

…of ANNE…

Strange things in earth be
came familiar –
figments honeycombed
actualised
sized up shockingly
without warning –
these things noisily alonged
vibrantly existed

membranes stranger
squatted
flared viral
acuity mangled senses –
squatted
smeared under
growth breathing visibly.

audibly. irregular. wiped.
glutinous cells against
naked ankles. nerve contractions.
revulsion.

families starved into strange creatures
otherworld animals –
eyelids sloughed and twitched for comfort
for food for fire
for quench

retina burnouts
scorch of contagious dreamscapes
parallel nightmares
beloved anaesthetic.

AKA ANNE REDFEARN

I remember my name
wafting like autumn
through the corridors of stone
and the occasional little pocket
of clarity.

It came curling round my body
securer with every repeated utterance
it fronds caressing with familiarity
constricting with unshakeable belonging.

Redfearn. So sticky. So brightly mine.
Until the book pressed shut.
Pressed out the light.
Dried up the sap.
And **I** vanished at the wave
of the nametakers.

...of THE BULCOCKS...

squeezing through gaps
 of hurt and backbreak
we travelled for miles –
    pressured by ripeness
                    by furious blood

(no genteel tittering larks
                    puckering lips to an 'O')

nagging at the hill
and hanging valleys
daft-mad with root spikes
& spirits
            piked with
feeling tangents

(till we cried)

AKA JANE BULCOCK & JOHN BULCOCK

Between the sigh and the
relief the floor caved
we danced on air
prematurely the
river was not human
northern clouds were stuffed
with hills and mountains –
the mother's son
the son's mother still.

Between the Not and the Guilty
they changed the rules
so anyone
could swing along to
non-sense
separate
the same
the related
at will
          a giftie bunch
we handed em that
          a bunch o bastards
we handed em that
and all the
fat earth wobbled
on its imaginary
axis.

...of SQUINTIN LIZZIE...

No, I was no beauty that's true
but with each telling my ugliness grows
like a bodily fungus
and guilt spreads accordingly
as though the two were somehow related.

How far has it spread now?
That my one dimensional
irreversible eye
could griddle spit at ten paces;
that no feckless speck of grit
daring to lodge in its deep
deformed corner could
hope to bring up a tear
or wipe away its malevolent glint.

And its counterpoint forming the unhappy alliance?
Cast in its asymmetrical role
roving over bodies, unrepentant,
turning stars and stomachs
throwing up fear upon aesthetic fear;
an obvious pool of iniquity.

Still, you've got to laugh, in fact,
in the twisted face of such poppycock
I could easily break into a cackle –
but I think the irony would allude you.

AKA ELIZABETH DEVICE

Your nightmares spilled over
and sucked me in.
Couldn't wake you.
No, couldn't wake myself but
the dead stirred slightly
on the third scream
and the days became dark
without centre
of sense.

One visit
to this reality
has been enough for me
with its ways and means
of making us
chalk words of desperation before
smashing the slate
clean into the face of
oncoming
dawns and all my born dreary days to this
ever nearing death of
laughable proportions.
This trumped up charge of nothing
to nowhere
but your fantasies of flight
and
ugly imaginings.

...of ALIZON...

Sure we dreamt charms:
stared into watery space making
ripples across the boredom
and piss-thin broth

and those sometimes dry summers
sinking head-low and happy in
grasses and bracken:
mating with ghosts.

Sure we made spells:
knees under chins toes wiggling
fingers doing silly dances knotting
hair in kiss curls

to the tock-a-tock mechanicals of stars
swopping giggle-gossip and riddles
till rain spat and scattered us
back to predictability.

AKA ALIZON DEVICE

I just dwindled into the situation
dwindled into life really
what alternative?
fourteen and female – an unloved combination

violence seemed futile

to smash the head and
fists
against an anger
a dungeon wall
bloodies only the moment
and yourself

a transient relief?
– not really –
an exchange of pain?
– not even that –
distraction
pure distraction

the situation still surrounds
reinforced – immovable
manacled
still there

the prating coxcombs
                    soft-brained rulers
indifferent nature
                    cynical history

ARE YOU LISTENING?

I said
I just dwindled in...
till late August...
shut my weary red-rimmed eyes...
dwindled out...

...of JAMES...

A weary life.
Vacancy sod. Perpetual damp.
Our very entrails fusted. Swoll.
And the nights:
Dead blue they goes. Lurid-like.
Glowy cold. Starved to each
poriferous bone. Aching warmth.
Aching feet creepin up between
Alliz inner thighs screamin
gedoff sob-laughin
(little Jenny joininin)
flailin daft-to-bleedin kicks
six seggy 'eels scouring dark
for blood heated landings
mother groanin shudup
moanin grow up please
to her self-soft sleep and
earth warm dirt
of her dreams –
as thirty little piggies
squealed demented
in extremis.

AKA James Device

I wasn't here I was here I won't
here I wasn't here I was here I
wasn't' was
here
today gone to
fora feeble
bit part
my tongue off on
off was was not
here was I was not I t-here I was here me
HEAR ME
w-here was why was
they was draggin me
to won't here along
to wasn't here my
part bit
snip-snippity
my strut kicked feeble
tongue lollery
lip-s-titched to-g
buggered and frog marcht t t-here
w-here I was not
HEARD

ALL SING

What was that jingle?

'Now the book is open spread
Now the writing must be read
Which condemns'
What did it mean?

The impenetrable is impenetrable
until penetrated:
the mind could not grasp this
but
the gentle downrush of a sigh
the (transfixing) power of pain
the absolute (   ) ness of pain
this
it could grasp:
memory became moment became memory
and the mouth opened wide with a shuddering
with a split / dawn / realisation
damming the vastness
utterness
out and outness
speechutter
word chains.

The mind could not
can not bear but
slidslides back into
trivia:
imbecilic elation
slippery tongues.

What was that jingle?

TOUCHING THE EVERYWHERE

THE ETERNAL BEWILDERMENT OF JENNET DEVICE

I weird sang. High trilled and skirled.
I led a merry crab dance. Bright.
Kookie-mad.
Rhymed thing with thing string...
word buntings   wildways
                            across
            XXXXXXXXXXXXX
For ever acting   ever playing
        all   out
The giggle-game trickled to the brink.

Oh ma
mi maa   mi mother
mUth   er   ing
muth   rin
muR   ther   ing   ringa
killything-a.   Gran.   Ali.   J.
killyall things bright
            XXXXXXXXXXXXX
killykin a killy killy-kin
ever mother mothering
(eat yer din-dins)

Below our rolling dream hills
rivers lisped unfunny with
tongue twist inquest

O mother mine
mother o me
mother o diva
mother o prima
diva-donna on the hill
sang
mother-O   me-O
O that
lime lit cherry glow
moment
table high and turning
mi heart content....

a turn of consequence unknown
till
slow and sinking in
till
known out loud

alone

Oh Ma
the word all round
is

TOUCHED